Dear Family,

What's the best way to help your child love reading?

Find good books like this one to share—and read together!

Here are some tips.

●**Take a "picture walk."** Look at all the pictures before you read. Talk about what you see.

●**Take turns.** Read to your child. Ham it up! Use different voices for different characters, and read with feeling! Then listen as your child reads to you, or explains the story in his or her own words.

●**Point out words as you read.** Help your child notice how letters and sounds go together. Point out unusual or difficult words that your child might not know. Talk about those words and what they mean.

●**Ask questions.** Stop to ask questions as you read. For example: "What do you think will happen next?" "How would you feel if that happened to you?"

●**Read every day.** Good stories are worth reading more than once! Read signs, labels, and even cereal boxes with your child. Visit the library to take out more books. And look for other JUST FOR YOU! BOOKS you and your child can share!

The Editors

For Krispy.
Thanks to my family, friends, and faith.
—DB
For Harry and Otto, for their tremendous support.
—AR

Text copyright © 2004 by Dalila Boyd.
Illustrations copyright © 2004 by Anna Rich.
Produced for Scholastic by COLOR-BRIDGE BOOKS, LLC, Brooklyn, NY
All rights reserved. Published by SCHOLASTIC INC.
JUST FOR YOU! is a trademark of Scholastic Inc.

Library of Congress Cataloging-in-Publication Data

Boyd, Dee.
  Only the stars / by Dee Boyd ; illustrated by Anna Rich.
    p. cm.—(Just for you! Level 2)
  Summary: Tia loves stars more than anything else and wishes to see them in the daytime,
too, so her grandmother helps her find ways to enjoy stars all day long. Includes activity
ideas for parents and children.
  ISBN: 0-439-56862-5 (pbk.)
  [1.Stars—Fiction. 2. Grandmothers—Fiction 3. African Americans—Fiction.] I. Rich,
Anna, 1956- ill. II. Title. III. Series.

PZ7.B69159On 2004
[E]—dc22
                                                              2004042907

10 9 8 7   09 10 11
        Printed in the U.S.A. 109 • First Scholastic Printing, February 2004

Only the Stars

by Dee Boyd
Illustrated by Anna Rich

Tia Johnson loved nighttime.
She loved the stars most of all.

One night, Tia made a wish.
She told it to her grandmother.

"I wish I could see the stars all the time,"
Tia said. "But every morning, they're gone!
Where do the stars go, Nana?"

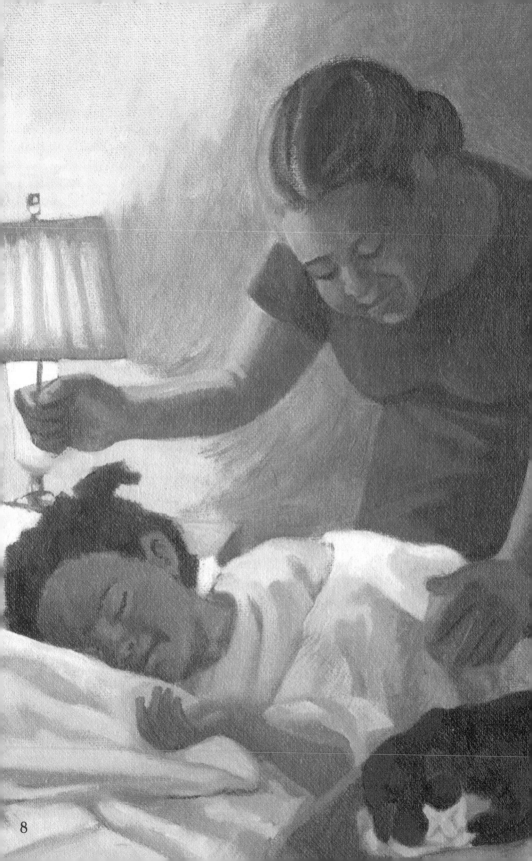

"We'll talk about it tomorrow,"
Nana said.
Then Nana turned out the light.
"Good night, Tia," she whispered.

The next morning, Tia woke up early.
She saw white clouds, a red bird,
and a pretty blue sky.
It was not as pretty without the stars.

At breakfast Tia asked,
"Where do the stars go
in the daytime, Nana?
You promised to tell me!"

"They're still in the sky, Tia,"
Nana said.
"You just can't see them."

After breakfast, Tia went back
to her room.
She pulled down a shade.
R-I-P!

Tia had pulled too hard!
Now there was a tear in the shade.
Sunlight shone through it.
"Hmmm," Tia said to herself.
She had an idea!

Tia got some black paper.
She got her crayons.
She ran to the kitchen
to tell Nana her idea.

Tia looked for scissors and tape.

Then she drew shapes on the black paper.

Nana cut them out.

What did they make?

Stars!

"Amazing!" said Nana.

That afternoon, Nana and Tia
went swimming at the lake.
The sun was so bright,
it hurt Tia's eyes.

"I know just what you need,"
said Nana.

Nana took Tia to the man
who was selling sunglasses.
She let Tia pick out a pair.

By the time they drove home, the sun
looked like a big orange ball.
"Soon we'll see the stars!" said Tia.

"We can see one right now," Nana said.
"The sun is a star that shines in the day.
It's much closer to Earth than any other star.
That's why it looks so big and bright."

Tia and Nana watched the sun go down.
It was as pretty as a sky full of stars.
"Amazing!" said Tia.

"Sometimes," Nana said, "you have what
you wish for without even knowing it!"

Here are some fun things for you to do.

That's Amazing!

Nana said the stars they made in Tia's room are **amazing**.

Amazing means surprising and wonderful.
Why do YOU think Nana said that?

Tia said the sun is amazing.
Why do YOU think she said that?

Look around your home. Look outdoors, too.
Do YOU see something surprising and wonderful?

Draw a picture of something amazing that YOU found.

Two Kinds of Stars

Tia loves the stars in the sky.
People can be stars, too!

A star is a person who is very
good at doing something!
Stars seem to shine brighter
than everyone else.

Some stars are great singers
or ballplayers.
Others are writers, artists,
or leaders.

Do you think YOU are a star at doing something?
How do YOU outshine everyone else?

Write a story about what it would be like to be a star.

▲▲▲▲TOGETHER TIME ▲▲▲▲

Make some time to share ideas about the story with your young reader!
Here are some activities you can try. There are no right or wrong answers!

Talk About It: Tia and Nana go swimming at the lake. Ask your child,
"What else do the pictures tell us about Tia and her grandmother? Are
there some other things they might like doing together?" What do you and
your child like to do on warm, sunny days?

Think About It: Tia loves to look at the sky! How does what we see in
the sky change from morning to night? How can changes in the weather
change the way the sky looks?

Read More: Was your child surprised to find out that the sun is a star?
Even though this story is made up, or fiction, what Nana tells Tia is fact.
Visit the nonfiction section of the library to find more books with facts
about the sun and stars.

Meet the Author

DEE BOYD says, "One night, I saw my cat Krispy sitting on the window sill, looking up at the night sky. I wondered if Krispy was admiring the stars. It got me thinking about summer vacations when I was a child, and how much I had loved watching the stars, too. That's how Tia's story began."

Dalila "Dee" Boyd grew up in New Jersey and later moved to Providence, Rhode Island, to attend the Rhode Island School of Design. She enjoyed living there so much that she decided to stay after she graduated from college. Today she works as an animator, illustrator, and writer. Dee began writing for children in part because she believes there is a real need for a wide variety of realistic stories about African-American children. *Only the Stars* is her first book.

▲▲▲▲▲▲▲▲▲▲▲▲▲▲▲▲▲▲▲

Meet the Artist

ANNA RICH says, "I have been drawing ever since I got hold of my first crayon. My mother was a kindergarten teacher—she knew the importance of crayons and paper! One of my other favorite activities is reading, so it's not surprising that I became an illustrator. I don't think I thought once about being anything else, except perhaps a writer. When I was about nine, I filled my composition books with stories that I wrote and illustrated. There were always lots of pictures!"

Anna has illustrated more than 20 books for children, including *Saturdays at the New You* by Barbara Barber and *Just Right Stew* by Karen English. She lives on Long Island, in New York, with her husband and son. Anna paints in a studio at home. She did the artwork for this book in oil on canvas. When she is not busy painting, Anna enjoys knitting and sewing.